P9-CEL-804

60¢ COFFEE AND A QUARTER TO DANCE

60¢ COFFEE AND A QUARTER TO DANCE

A POEM

JUDY JORDAN

LOUISIANA STATE UNIVERSITY PRESS

BATON ROUGE 2005

Manufactured in the United States of America
FIRST PRINTING

DESIGNER: Barbara Neely Bourgoyne
TYPEFACES: Adobe Minion, text; House Painter Sign Showcard, display
PRINTER AND BINDER: Edwards Brothers, Inc.

Grateful acknowledgment is made to the editors of the following publications, in which portions of this poem have appeared, sometimes in different versions: *Alaska Quarterly Review* (2002), *Blue Pitcher* (1992), *Gulf Coast* (2003), *Perigee: A Publication for the Arts* (2001), and the *Southeast Review* (2004).

LIBRARY OF CONGRESS CATALOGING-IN-PUBLICATION DATA
Jordan, Judy, 1961–
Sixty-cent coffee and a quarter to dance : a poem / Judy Jordan.
p. cm.
ISBN 0-8071-2995-X (alk. Paper) — ISBN 0-8071-2996-8 (pbk. : alk. paper)
I. Title. II. Title: 60-cent coffee and a quarter to dance.
PS3560.O7295S59 2005
811'.54—dc22

2004029938

The paper in this book meets the guidelines for permanence and durability of the Committee on Production Guidelines for Book Longevity of the Council on Library Resources. ♾

PROLOGUE

In winter's spider-eyed light strung through steam grates, the tunnels turn feral.
This is the other city, the dark one
of hidden passages, runaways and orphaned days

and like me it sleeps in broken buildings
and smells of a sad suicide from the fifteenth century, and like me
it has smoked three things on the mold-furred walls

which are the only altars
of those who've dropped through holes in the sidewalk
to descend to these steam tunnels rung by slick rung.

This city shambles room to room.
Drawn to the easy sound of sleep,
it knows the pattern night pens on tender skin,

knows your darkest secrets and tells
no one except the sycamore
which rips from its skin with shame.

It wants absolution,
taps your sins on water pipes to shudder out of faucets,
ties them to the tail feathers of soot-mottled birds

who beat up from the concrete-lipped curb,
falter over cars, stutter
then catch an oily gust and wheel into the scalded sky.

It claims to be blind though it might have a thousand eyes,
screams obscenities from 13th and University and pisses in alleys.
Sometimes it drinks too much. Sometimes it begs for more.

It hides tents among trees in the park by the sluggish river
this red-eyed thing blinking from storm grates.
It is a window breaking.

Other people's blood in its veins, skin on fire,
smack, crack, meth, strychnine and scouring powder sold as speed,
some drug or another telling it die, you must die. But it doesn't die.

Step around it on your way to the theater.
It crawls through your bedroom window, a warm bed and in the morning
the smell of coffee and bacon spitting in grease. That's all it wants.

Aching hands in underwear drawers,
snagged silks.
You are its worst nightmare.

Coiled cable, blood and razor-wire, shredded muscle and blue bone,
cold nights, the city under the city
is where you'll find me. Though not now.

Now it is heat-hazed summer and sunset
and I whisper the four-syllable name of the stranger
I should have become and disappear through the back door

of the Villa Inn where the cook paces the few feet
between the makeline and the ovens
muttering *Chimbukee*   *Chimbukee*   *Chimbukee*

It's been nine years since he's known the burned light
of his own country or a woman's name churned in sea foam, nine years
since he's clung to flesh which smells of rosemary and dried tomatoes.

He checks his billfold, thick with this week's pay. *Let's go*
he says to me, pointing toward his apartment across the alley.
Let's go Super Ju. Party. Party, he says

then reaches his swollen hands deep into his pants
past the flour-grubbed belt line
and with a hard twist adjusts his truss.

We call him Chris though that's not his name
and I think to myself, Homer, Odysseus,
the blood-blue sea, the sun in its relentless veracity

be damned to hell and back. Sweating pizza drivers, me sleeping
in my truck or if it's winter in empty buildings and the steam tunnels,
and every weekend the parking lot filling up with dope dealers

with their out-of-state plates
and hookers dropped off by their pimps
and the homeless who stumble

from the boarded buildings and doorways to this oiled kaleidoscope
under the warehouses' dark windows—
the broken, fish-line-strung and eye-level hooked—

this grease-barrel and sour dumpster-stinking,
trash-can-blaze, busted bottles, pissed on pissed off
fuck you fuck you kill strong-armed ambulance scream, parking lot

and Chris saying *Chimbukee*   *Chimbukee*   *Chimbukee*
cussing us, *Scata. Malaka American. Sto dyavolo malaka,*
Pizza malaka. Deliver, Chris yells but slow night

no orders, no tips so we yell back, *You malaka.*
Give us pizzas. To kríma sto lemó sou, Chris says
Greek which to us means nothing.

and just outside the fish-net stockinged, stiletto-heeled
Star, Joy, Princess. Joy, I think, and am too tired to think anything else
when she tells me she swings, asks if I have something,

anything, coke, smack, speed, rock. *At least some pot. Come on. Hook me up,* she says.
Then the teams. Salt & Sugar. Salt & Pepper. Nilla & Chocolate
with their matching tattoos, Comedy & Tragedy. Happy one day, Dead the next.

Angel, Love Boat, Crystal.
I got first degree   I got MG
Blue ludes, 8-Balls, rocks, the dealers yell.

Quiver & Shiver   Come
get my stash   I got the stuff
Tongo & Cash

Lot of Candy Man & Sweet Stuff.
Slick the Stick, a pimp caught up in his own rhyme.
Lover Boy & Philly Boy. Wanna-be's and gonna-be's:

60¢ COFFEE AND A QUARTER TO DANCE

I don't want to know but it's night
and under streetlights the color of foil
the thin-skinned moths call our names
telling us to keep in sync,
to write our prayers, mark our paths,
to remember their wings, to not fall.

Yet they fall. Tracing scant trails of flame
they are sounds to lean into,
lean and swirl, down
and down under the black netting,
falling, falling, unfurled,
we lean and swirl,
under the jointed stars, under the broken,
throbbing, many-eyed, cold and lidless stars:

....

Stone-dry light of late afternoon,
sun flaming out over pines
as one by one the road's mirages heavy with heat
surrender to the slate night and buzz of city streets.

Deli and drugstore, Villa Inn and the one-eyed grease joint
crammed under the eleven-dollar-a-night apartments
all shadowed into bas-relief by the hospital's coal chimneys.

This evening, rise through taverns of pain to my day:
to memory and the strangeness of ambulance-flash
in the black-ribbed night, the world quavered in red light
swinging out then back, and the woman
who only two weeks ago, her naked body sprawled
along the railroad tracks, dead from an overdose
but raised again to common light
and ordinary world, is again dead.

This time she remains. Her eyeless self fully embraced,
she lies down to the eternity
of stories told over and over,
even the dead trying to get it right,
even they failing in the blood-lush way only they can.
Restless they are in their mistakes, cramped in their tunnels of worms.

But what do we care, curled here,
stumbling toward our own bruised futures.
Larry on the kitchen steps bent across the Carolina Blues:
Fighting in public. Ninety days, the judge said, *Pea farm.*
Early spring and nothing but peas, row after row,
miles of peas struggling toward a heat-hazed horizon.
Here I am, he hums, the beginning of that row no closer than the end.
Plowed and planted, hoed and picked and canned.
The other boy paid his fine, Larry moans to the six strings.
Prison work farm and nobody eats tonight, he sighs

while Steve holds vigil over pus and swell,
days after pulling a knife's ragged blade
up his own forearm. Maybe this time
he'll climb the twenty-three steps
through the crown of his oil-clumped head
rung by fevered rung and swing into the blistered sky.
At least this should be good for a week in the hospital
where the 3 a.m. squeaky-shoed nurses finger
a cool sigh against his burning skin.

And John, he's drunk, students drunk,
dishwasher, drivers, and two cooks, all drunk.
John falling out of his chair, távla sto meϑeési, under the table,
to bed with a shovel, too drunk to drink, pie-eyed drunk:

Tiny John works all week, drunk all weekend
and with nowhere else to go
hangs out in the kitchen of the Villa
and says to nobody, *I love my mama.*

I don't care what they say, I'm gonna call her someday.
Drunk or sober I'm gonna call her.

Kookoo he says to Chris,
meaning *kukla*—darling—*Get me a beer.*

Me léne Kóstas, Chris says. *Me léne Kóstas.*

....

Go ahead Chris, tell me. A little boy in Greece
barefoot and dust-coated in that time of starvation
is how I imagine you. On every corner soldiers
eating their crusty bread and sausages of blood
dropping crumbs for the sport of watching children fight.
Their raucous songs followed you through the narrow streets
and climbed the knotted rosemary to your window
where nightmares sank their teeth
into the shell's echo you felt you had become
then swallowed you like a rogue wave.

But it is not what you remember but what you cannot forget.
Not the town you left behind
nor the street you walked each day
but the street that is no longer there
in the town which is now a field
in a sun-struck stretch of field after field.

Maybe you were a knock-legged, skinned-kneed boy
tending goats in a rocky land outside of Missolonghi
living on goat milk and goat meat and boiled weeds.
You walked terraced fields wondering what happened to the gods
in a place where everything had its season
and goats determined the season.

Or maybe you lived in Macedonia on the upper floor
of a house on pillars. The sea visited twice each day,
emptying itself out and filling again
while you fished from the veranda
and green water snuffled up your first-floor walls.

Fish bumped in the bucket at your feet
until you leaned over the railing and tumbled
them back to the sea—mica-flaked Lazaruses—
and you a small god in a country of man-sized gods.

Later you'd study the walls and the sea's fevered marks,
muddy tracks and froth and spurf's cursive
licking toward where you had stood on the floor above;
a palimpsest, meaning something you were sure
even if you didn't know what.

In this city you saw your first Germans
goose-step through with their iron teeth and marbled eyes

and here the water brought you the first
of your many dead. Still in their soiled uniforms,
they listed for hours on the flat sea
and slowly spilled into your back yard.
To écho se kakó.
An omen, a bad, bad omen.

Maybe I've got it all wrong:
you lived on an island
a day's boat ride from the mainland.
Andros perhaps with its narrow, winding streets,
Naxos bustling and blue-shuttered.

When day came, it was as fish and salt,
an indescribable light and the gas-stink of boats.
You waited on the beach with the oldest men repairing nets
trying to stitch sense into that thing called war,
tracing its cross strands and knots to some beginning,
the way you would a pirate map's series of riddles,
but each cord and hatch led you only
to the roil of birds and waves,
fish, and a light so impossible it was painful.

Finally the morning your father touched you awake and said *today*
then your hands callus-yellow, curled to the shape of the oars.

Here you learned to navigate absence
of wind and stars, learned sea swells and shoals,
the way one current will work with you
while the undercurrent undoes everything.

You climbed into craters that stank of sulfur,
swam in water heated by earth's fire,
watched from near hills when the first archaeologists
sank shovels in volcanic ash centuries old.
Akrotiri you said, letting the two hard consonants
slam against your mouth's roof while the vowels
floated from deep in your throat to July's heat.
The Lost Atlantis you said, unsurprised
for what could surprise you in a country
where gods still take tea
and play castanets in cloud-studded mountain-tops.

....

Somewhere in the barn owl's shadowed slide
across the last slivered glint of moon,
huddled with the mice in the centuries' debris,
dried grass and broken pillars, I find fragments—

guttered phrase, a nod where there should be no nod,
and as I have with my own animal-furied life,
I search for that which will give us all names.

I've heard it theorized we're nothing but language
                                                                                    but I don't think so
unless we're also determined by a word's absence,
my father punishing us, not talking for weeks,
or something concrete as cholera, 156 hogs dead,
the weeks of quarantine,
my father drunk again, fired again.

Maybe the lack of something as simple as a syllable
piled the children into the split-pea green Plymouth
and drove them to Miss Pauline's
while five miles up the road
our house burned for the insurance,
                                                                but I don't think so.

Maybe there is traceable logic in my mother wrapping her disguised voice
around the phone, begging Louise Stegall to quit
that man, he was no good, that man whose life
before year's end would bleed out in Louise's carport.
Maybe some word that would've stopped Louise from killing him,
would have kept her from the institution.

And what could I have done if I'd known
how soon my mother would die, how I'd never forget
her words, telling me to scrub harder,

me on my knees in Louise's carport in puddled blood
that never did come up.

It's a type of loneliness,
a southern farm or a dazzling stretch of bare rock somewhere in Greece
but something more when what I reach for semaphores from the birds,
runs circles on the waste-slick asphalt,
then scuttles, foam-mouthed, under the cars,
something else when you're kissed by death's tongueless mouth.
As you know. As you know.

Shut up. Scase. Scata. Kópanos. All Americans malaka, you say
but it's what there are no words for which lies between us

despite all my nights which have limped into days I had betted against,
times I've joined strangers and we've emptied our pockets
of lint and bottle caps and made the sixty cents, sharing coffee refills
to stay awake at the corner table.
The jukebox only a quarter and if we'd had it, we might have danced,
shuffling between tables across the puzzle of pressed pine floor
while the two vets covered napkin after napkin
with poems about sunsets colored agent orange,
skies agent white and blue, color blasted from all the leaves,
all the leaves fluttering to the ground.

In today's heat the parking lot reeks of burnt flesh
and I walk pitched forward dragging one leg
or the other, the busted discs' shifts,
tunneled roots of rot-wasted pain
but what is that,
what is it
when it's a red, red rain and all over Greece
bodies claw from earth to raw air.

Though I've never palmed salt for the utter need to taste anything
or whipped the thumb of creamer to my traitorous mouth,
I have gone days without food,
fisted river dirt and eaten grit and sand,
grabbed bread crusts off deserted plates,
slumped to the corner table with my tenth refill

but in Athens that first winter
children fought for an olive stone
spat out by a German soldier
and the starved lay on the streets for hours
then were flung in the mass graves.

And on all the platforms all the quarry-carved and pit-eyed guards.

So I've brushed my teeth in public bathrooms,
slept in abandoned buildings, and carried
all I owned slung in a backpack—

this story and that, yours and mine,
but just words,
                    just words
which never quite touch,
   though they try, yes they try.

....

It is with needle and ink the hour before lights out
that I tell this story of America:
Princess bent over her left hand
her cellmate carving a cross in the web of flesh
between forefinger and thumb
and later Princess on the streets again
her needle-scarred skin, syringe of blood,
fire-rush of it through her veins,
faded cross and on her shoulder's blade
a heart, the initials D and B, the same blurred blue.
But what story is this, she hunched against
the brick buildings, the smokestacks
and the boxcar's lonely clicking.
A story precise as a machine, empty as black windows,
story of gutters and moldy cellars
and what lies under the city
with the muscled cords of telephone lines
and hollow entrails of sewer slime and gas pipes,
hundreds of miles of dry coughs and slag,
scorched copper and iron calling into the echoing dark,
Princess waiting above it all,
shirt riding up over the blank eye of her navel,
smoke from her cigarette
rising sure as an angel toward eternity.

1. Remembering & again I'm the child pretending

2. sleep, another man with my mother on the other side of the thin wall, not even an arm's length if I could push through this painted sheet of paste & paper, the fourth tonight, & as I listen, as I crawl from bed, as I churn from my room to hers, as I watch, so close, & do nothing, he hits her again

3. & again, & she is quiet & she is still & after a long time so is he.   Police come.   I don't remember   if he had a mustache, if his hair was blonde or brown

4. don't remember   anything but that I watched, that when he ran from the room some of her fell from his hands, a red splotch beside my pink footed Minnie mouse sleeper, &   I did nothing.

5. I clutch my doll, & the short story of my life has nowhere to go—my father   I don't know. Maybe it was that man,   stumbling down the narrow, stinking hall. Any of them who she led in every night while I played the sleep-game.

6. Then it was the orphanage.

7. I was six when the state found me a new set of parents.

8. Listen.

9. I don't worry about getting pregnant. Oh yeah my adopted father took care of that. Before I ever hit the streets; that's what the infection he gave me did. Had a hysterectomy at twelve; social workers took me back to the orphanage.

10. At night in the pale light roaches as thick as minutes crawled the walls, rats clamored from the sewers under the bloated moon & ate our dreams & the bedbugs didn't drown but did the backstroke in the pans of water we kept the bed legs in.

11. Tell me what else I could have done; old at twelve, I traded the shelter, the piss-stinking halls, the retarded girl tied in her chair & wet with vomit, the head mistress, mean as anything on the streets.

12. My father's daughter after all.

13. It's the same thing all of us are saying. The same words; they just all come out different.

14. Yeah crack revs my brain, blows its horn & grinds its gears but that's not what it's all about 'cause all the rocks in the world can't bust those windows, all the sugar in the tank can't stop that engine. It follows me on these sidewalks; everything I want pressing its heavy mouth against mine, wrapping me in its hundred green arms.

....

Through the streetlight-lit night and the truck's dirty pane
the coming storm and all it touches could be anything.

That tree for instance, is it a pitch pine or an Allegheny Chinquapin
one thick limb like an arm raised in air
beside a tangle of limb and leaf which the randomness

of the windy dark and my mind's leaps
twists into a happy doughboy face

until the truck shudders again in gusted wind
then branches and leaves squeeze into a demonic clown
from some movie I might have seen once.

Happy doughboy. Demon clown. The truck shivering
and shrinking further into itself against the storm

and all the time that tree's one arm waving, waving, saying what
to the swollen and sputtering night, to the cloud scuds
dropping from the formless sky toward the beaten earth.

Never mind about my being homeless; at least I have my pickup—
the indifferent protection of bug-smear and rust.

Just don't think about it; just don't.
We all need something in which we can wrap ourselves.
That tree; after all it's just waving good-bye.

. . . .

There will be day here but it's hard to remember
slumped in the shadows of shadows
in a fight for a one-eyed sleep.
Strange to know that with the first scream of birds
I will see that only yards from where I scrunch
in the front seat of my pickup are houses.

Strange to wake
to a six-battery, steel migraine-maker,
lighted blindness
and the shift and creak of four policemen
knocking on my truck window.
From sleep to the humiliation of being homeless

in a dark so thick nothing makes its way through
certainly not their words, not their *move on, move on.*

Drive, they said. Toward the hospital. Somewhere
else, where they're used to folks like you

because here is the river and vines grow so fast
a night's sleep lifts you to the tree tops.
Because here birds wake you
with syrupy tongues in your ears
and grasshoppers have forgotten how to spit.

The screams of feral cats make you forget your own mama,
souls clamber out peaks of heads
and tumble into the night sky.

Because trumpets sing back to the hummingbirds,
the railroad tracks to trains, bridge pilings to the river.
Because each spring people lose their back yards
and hushed days later find them again
damp and mussed, holding up the river's gifts.
        Because lightning never strikes.
        Not once, not twice
        not if you own a featherbed
nor if you sleep on moss and leaves
and the wood floors' sweet crumble of death and rot.

Here clocks run backward
    if they run at all
and baroque woodwork of 1800s' porches
calls your name as young gnomes creep from basements.

Because the Priest left the area three months ago
causing snails to shift onto their hard rumps,
their tendrils swaying in delight,
because snails know all answers but no riddles
and refuse to say who whispers in the smother of night,

refuse to say if the maggots will ever finish their never-ending task,
refuse to say, in the roots' shift and the grubs' sleep,
what the dead hold to the 'O' of their mouths.
And that river; it just keeps chasing
its own gritted dreams downstream.

. . . .

Move on, the policeman said, *move on*

when what I want is sycamores
the glass-eyed moon resting in their branches.
But here I spin in the slick sweat of an unreachable notion.
John, he spins too. Caught in the endless loop
of the ever-present past which is never made right
no matter how many times he twists the words around it
slurring again, *I don't care what they say,*
I'm gonna call her someday. Drunk or sober,

gonna call her. But who will I call
when what I want is the silver branches of birch
feathered in feral light, pale buds shivering in a skittish wind

even as John slobbers on,
love my mama, gonna call her
and outside the shouting grows louder

A fight A fight
a spic & a white
If the spic don't win
we all jump in

What is it I've carried for years
like seeds through a drought
into thin-sneakered winters,
pack of saltines, can of milk,
nights fighting sleep over sixty-cent coffee?

I want those nights to stop looking at me with the face of today,
want Chris to talk about the ocean's heaving,
wind in mountains which lift bulk-shouldered above cirrus cloud.
I want him to talk about his own heaving,
wind that blows heavy against his shoulders

but how can he when John keeps begging beer
and the fight outside moves closer:

Don't call your sister or your brother
Don't go crying to your mother
Better call your daddy
& hope he's able and ready.

Say that it was as I imagine:
the wondrous sun, endless sand, and tubs of salted fish.
Say basil and rosemary and the rough smell of brine,
machines, and ocean filling the air,
olive trees lined like marching soldiers,
broken boats tangled in red nets at the wet world's edge.

Say that you watched the men night fishing
and wondered how anyone who saw the lanterns' lights
mirrored and multiplied in ocean and sky
could not know that it was the gods of the cloud-cloaked mountains
come down to dance with the gods of the sea.

Want to know but where do words hide
here in the scant light of the kitchen,
tin cans stacked to the ceiling
blocking the scrap of a window thick with soot.
Here where the only sounds are the whoosh of the dishwasher,
the cooks' curses, and the fight outside the back door:

Now Mister Cracker
What you gonna do
Don't matter if you win or lose
We coming after you

Onomázome Kóstas, Chris says. *Onomázome Kóstas.*

Scaseh re. Scata. Malaka American, scaseh, Chris says.
It's real when it happens to you, the bumpersticker says
and the children sang, *Ashes, Ashes, we all fall down.*

Tell me: Do your dead also form ranks and stand at attention?
Do they continue their habits as in life;
this one arguing that the water from the Edesseos Valley
was so thick it had to be eaten with a spoon,
your mother loving the second pressing of olive oil
sprinkled over plum tomatoes and your sister crying for figs.

Did you grow up on an island so crowded
the dead jostled for position?
Are your dead like mine, listening
for their names in your stories?

Everyday they walk to the beach
certain the ocean will bring them some news,
sure they hear in the waves' whispers
something that sounds like *you live, you and you.*

I want to know did you ever have a hint
at how amazingly the past keeps up with you,
how it waits in the furred belly of the haunted
wood-lice plucked from Gabriel's wings,
how it marks today with blue graveyard lights,
sears its many names into your body,
twitches into its other selves,
waits, whimpering, under the bed.

I want to know what it is that is yet to come
this thing we carry in our bodies
cherished like all the promises we never heard
cupped to ourselves like a charm,

want to know when I am pinioned under death's ragged wing,

shorn and sinking through each hoarded memory,
what am I to do with these condemned years,

want to sleep tonight, tomorrow, sometime again
without the pounding of those policemen at my truck window,
want my eyes to know true dark
after waking blind, a six-battery head-knocker,
an eighteen-inch steel light pointed straight at me.

Move on, the policemen said, *Move on*

Want to walk without regret through the steam
from the fresh-washed streets
as the stray dogs drag out the night
and the river of rose oil remembers me,

want to not care that I'll never be found,
to follow the trail lined with dragonfly tails,

to be swept to fog's island
where no one's story will reach me
though they reach me now, as they should, they reach me now.

....

1. I saw that in the world of hookers, street walkers, working girls, whores, pimps, tricks, & johns, we lived by a strict code: protect each other, trust no one. No, especially not yourself.

2. Nobody had friends only other hookers who'd watch your back.

3. It was too late by the time I saw how nobody ever left that life, saw how it didn't look good on your pimp, saw how he'd track you down & kill you rather than let you go.

4. But she was special.

5. She was my friend.

6. Me & her, we was gonna get jobs. On the outside.

7. This is just what happened. That's all. Nothing else.

8. One night a man came & he kept coming & always with the same magazine & always open to the same centerfold & always saying it was her.

She said no she wouldn't pose in the crotchless red string bikini he brought, said no to the lacy bra, no to his money, though he kept saying the centerfold posed for anyone who bought that magazine why not she for him & all she could say was no because he was crazy

9. which he was.

10. I was catty corner & a block away the night he came with a gun.

11. We all came running—every street walker, whore, working girl, stomp-down, mud-kicking ho & hooker in a scream's distance—cracked up, cracked out, just plain cracked, if it was screaming distance, it was running distance,

12. but it was too late.

13. Me & her pimp went to the police. They said for us to go home; come back when we got the needles out our arms.

14. Me & Slick. We looked all night but it was the police who stumbled on her scrunched up in a fist of arms & knees & dried blood, her head pressed real tight & her ear all flat against the floorboard in the trunk of a beat-up car in a beat-up parking lot. Don't go asking what she was listening for. Don't even. She wasn't hearing nothing.

....

The years of occupation,

the public square where the twenty
from your village waited.

Twenty was it?   Forty?   Sixty.   A hundred.   Dressed
up.   They waited.   They scraped,

hands   and   knees,   across   the truck's oil-scummed boards.
Carrying their one bag.   Carrying
their old,   their sick,   their

what,   where they were going.

East.   To Cracow   soldiers

said.   Your friend's mother   worrying
Cracow Jews spoke a different dialect.

Huddled   in their rheumy coats and their yellow stars.

Waited   with their bundles.   Boarded.

Attention! All Jews! Attention!
A loudspeaker howled through cobbled streets.

The street rutilant with sun,
you held pebbles in your mouth against hunger
while soldiers grew oily with food.

Maybe all television and books, my own favored myths
tucked under my tongue, words edgy as blades,
is all I'll hear but I want to know the fields
where once had been towns, hand-written signs:

Here once was the village of ——
and for miles nothing but weeds and thirsty land.

Or the hand-lettered cardboard that says
here in Serres were 600 Jews.

Before the war.

After there were three.

Here in Didimotica there were 900.

After there were 33.
Here in Kalávryta there were men and there were boys,
696 old men, baby boys.

Now there are none.

I would like to know what it was for you to walk
with wind under the hard and bilious sun
after reading what was written on the field's edge:

Here was Komeno, town of 317 farmers and fishermen,
women and men and children.

What it is to know what the sign does not say:

Six hours of machine-guns and cannon fire and flames.

Fibrous wind, flinty sun
and that place they threw the dead.

Even the soldiers were sickened by what they'd done.

Not that I could ever know for it's all in your language,
you may talk and talk and talk, to me your words mean nothing.

....

Everywhere broken marble that at one time led to a city.
Broken marble and an endless stretch of empty plain.
Thousands of years and still this marvelous lack.

The road ends at the cross on the north slope of Tremola above Kalávryta
where it is always December and always 1943
and the hands on the church clock have stopped at 2:34.

No men in this village.
No men and no boys.
Only women in black walking in the snow-silence,

in the silence that will never be after the machine-gun-silence,
in light crosshatched with drifting snow
under clouds the color of warm milk.

It is these clouds the dead raise
in their cupped hands to quench their unquenchable thirst.

....

Tell me Chris are there nights long after the sun's
yolk has broken across the mountains' blue ridge
when time becomes so bold it crawls its way
from hibernation and shimmies naked
and shivering to the trees' highest branches,
when the river weeps so loud and long
the fish choke on their own old sorrows,
when the wild onions close their eyes one by one
and the Queen Anne's Lace fold up
their blood-spotted handkerchiefs
and lie down in ditch weed and sorrel the final time,
nights when the steel band of your ribs tightens
and your hands go cold, nights when you know
you will never see Greece again. Never.

....

If it's true that violent death gives rise to ghosts
then all the world is haunted and Greece especially
floats above itself, life in death, death in life, a blue netherworld
in which every day you said good-bye to someone else
and when it was your father, were you there
to hear him cry, *Oh what have they done?*
Did his last breath hang about his face
and was the air in the room suddenly gone as if a blast
had ripped through it like in the graveyard Turk soldiers tore
up for their houses. Your house, garden, people, all gone,
your father mumbling about the ceramic roof, red-tiled,
terraced yard, and begging for an orange.

I'm sorry papa; oranges don't grow there anymore
Oranges don't grow

. . . .

Did I eat grass, wild greens that grew between railroad tracks?
    Am I a cow, to have eaten grass?
Wait beneath windows, German officers tossing apple cores
to the street? Apple cores we feed our goats, our pigs.
My blood boils in my body. No soldier
left it spattered on kitchen walls.
Did I eat cat? Only those in the hospital had meat.

Standing in line for rationed bread, wormy peas.
Commander Pasha boasting he'd collected barrels of salted
ears to send back to Turkey? Ten barrels. Different war.
Years before. Cicadas calling their litany of thirst and pain
from the eucalyptus trees. Did I walk the streets to the hospital
to see if my cat's orange-striped skin hung there?
It was war, World War, then another they called Civil.
Saying good-bye to one person, then another, trucks and garbage carts
in the night picking up the dead piled in front of houses. What people
did I have to say good-bye to? I had no friends, no tiger-striped cat:

....

Athens, February, 1942, sitting
on the wooden step, streets empty
when you touch my knee.
Lead balloons pour from your mouth
and rise to the steel underbelly of the sky.

So you have died my friend.
Scratched from yourself, stretched out on the street,
raisins forced between your lips.
Now you wear a wreath of ilex
and carry a string of rats' heads slung across your back.

You were always the generous one
but I know better than to eat food
offered by the dead and cross my fingers
against the omen of you and your meal of rats.

So now you are just one more soul
zigged open by the blue light of hunger
and handed over to the indifferent care of the gods.

Death has whittled you razor-edged.
It has whittled me too only I am not dead.
Unbelieving I say this out loud.

Flares like glow worms crawl from my mouth,
my hands turn to spades and you say *There are graves to be dug.*

Have you nothing more to say when only last month we bled
wrist to wrist and joined the packs of children grounging
the rocks of Hymettus for horta, dinner's grass and weeds.

It's a new day. There is no forgiveness.

ELAS guerrilla, thirteen years old, 1943
and night, that hungry executioner, letting down his ropes;
I open my mouth to cry out
but barbed wire spools from deep in my throat.

Miserias, the sausage-skinned man,
tells me he loves me but his tangled beard
grows hands and each one holds my burning heart.

The nightmares. Again.
It was the boy we killed today
who spat up blood and wire,
the length of it run through him
and he thrown against the wind-blasted rocks.

The War God I call *Kapetanios*
said it had to be, that the boy's father
collaborated with capitalists, that he helped the British
blow up a German-held railroad bridge.

I pull my sheepskin rug tighter
and crawl out into the reeling dark.
I find the boy and lie down on top of him.
Hold still, I say. *I'll keep you warm*
but he pushes from the rocks
and we lift into the snow-swirled night.
I squeeze him tighter but he shatters
like crystal, his blood blooming into poppies
that fall to the Antares hiding below.

In the morning Miserias kneels beside me,
takes my rag-wrapped feet in his hands and calls me son.
His bloody face is the blinding, black cavern of my dreams.
I close my eyes to keep from tumbling
into the stretched stone of that sky.

After the planes there was always a sliced
moment between the bombs and the noise of bombs

when everything held   as if waiting

before the buildings sucked in the diesel-scummed air
like a chest-shot man sucks in breath

then finally, slowly, crumbled toward the earth.

Once in the brick-fall, dust-rise, scream and wind-swirl
I tumbled out of the world

to everything snagged to a stuttered stop.

The falling houses and buildings, the rising dust and debris,
the sirens and shooting and screams all stopped.

I walked through that stillness to the world's edge

where I saw that even the water had risen
and not fallen and waited

with the one wave forever slashed across the shore

and the man who lay there
looking as if he had just flung himself

onto the beach and pulled up his shirt to the sun

when the water washed over his body
and did not begin its slow pulling away.

The blood-roiled and oily wave holding

above his head, holding like a dark scar across the sand,
across the one man who is there still, so still.

I am through with the nightly folding of Greece
like each day's stale dishtowels.

Through with the streets filling up with the dead
so many so fast they could not be buried.

Through with the gathering of bodies.
Up and down our streets all night they called

Bring us your dead. Have you any dead?
as if they were peddling fish

except there was no fish, no food at all.
Through with the smell of burning flesh

like fried chicken filling our pores. Through with everything
smelling like meat frying. Through with it.

And the hunger, curling into ourselves
our joints growing large under our thin skin,

the dead, blood and bone and muscle strewn in the street,
feral cats eating the brains.

On my walk to school I saw this.
I'm through with it.

And all the dogs long gone, even the rats gone
and my friend telling me that after a bombing

he found a hand. Just a hand.
He and his mother and young brother ate it.

I asked which hand;
I wished I could find the other.

I'm through with it.

I have no answer for the dry stream beds,
for the black cyprus and the gnarled fig,

no answer for the rocks and rubble
or the pillars as they strike against the stark sky,

no answer for the bodies that rise
each year closer to the surface,

nothing for the blood that ran in the streets
or for those thrown from the cliffs to the sea.

It is they who choose to eat eel and flat fish,
they who call octopus a delicacy.

Where the sea lies flat in unbearable light
then turns in on itself shifting, gibbous, indigo to blue stone,

go there and ask the sea what it says.
What the sea answers I answer.

Imagine us then   a people pared down
to flight   to the things we left behind
dropped in the road   to bone   to hunger

Don't think of my mother just beyond
the door   turned away   bent
over shrubs of rosemary
the sun glancing off her shears
the silent horizon stretching from her
Don't think of my father his cigarette stubbed
like a sore in the corner of his mouth

Don't give me memories
to sicken me with their lies

Some times do not bear remembering

Can you imagine a people who died
faster than they were born?

Think of black bread and sawdust
the fields grown empty

Imagine nets to be mended
imagine the world needing mending
Imagine children inventing their own lives
and weaving those inventions through days
that will never be mended

A city of thieves   a city of dying   imagine that
we held rags across our face against the smell
but there was no keeping out that winter of evil

isyo   skaza   chano   afandos

Imagine what you will but do not imagine me

What is the word for justice   for escape
for lost?   Disappear?

If there is a word for never
can you ever know it
if hope
dare we speak it?

....

1. I was young then. If a hooker could be young.

2. Didn't have no pimp. Paid SlewBoy to protect me.

3. No pimp & plenty of money. Fur coat. Diamond watch. Steak every night.

4. Protection? Baby, somebody's got to watch your back.

5. That night they grabbed me off the corner of 11th & Tuscarawas, I screamed for SlewBoy. Screamed

6. & kept screaming. Right through the huge knuckled hand in my mouth, through the needle's jab & the blaze up my arm & its hundred-tongued leap to my head. Kept screaming while I lay slash-scarred by light from the barred bit of window against the ceiling high above my head. Screamed as more drugs dragon-blazed or limped scaly-armed & slimy through my body, then screamed more when there weren't no more drugs. Screamed when the men came, lines of them, one by one, unbuckled their pants. Then went away.

7. Them men? Nothing. Just more training.

8. SlewBoy knew all about it. It was him that sold me to PhillyBoy.

9. Nothing but training.

10. PhillyBoy took me to The Golden Pheasant. The waitress brought drinks. Philly threw my drink across the room.

11. The waitress brought SlewBoy a cheeseburger. He always ordered extra cheese & a pickle.

12. Philly said to me, *I could kill you. I could kill me anybody. I done took care of plenty before you.* Philly pointed at his Doberman & said, *That's my dog. He's trained. Like you gonna be.* Then he said to that dog, *Lick her.* Then he said, *fuck her.*

It's just what happened. It ain't nothing else.

13. No. Now you listen here. It was in the front room of the Pheasant. Everybody saw it. Anybody could have walked in & that wouldn't have made a gnat's ass of difference.

14. You got it girl. Training.

....

A smart mouse can learn a complicated maze
in ten seconds flat
& though Jimmy says the pizza driver
is nothing more than a mouse
scurrying the city for our reward of another delivery,
we're not nearly so fast—

taking the bait again & again
& chewing off our own feet
though we make excellent pets
& witches only add our brains to potions of love
when newts & salamanders can't be found.

When one mouse quits his job
all the mice rush to the waitress' station
& lick the little butters
& gulp down coffee without shoes or socks,
which is what country mice call black coffee,
until fur singes & brains cook.
The mouse who escapes from the toothed
& cheese-loaded wild, gets the job.
He is glaze-eyed with glee,
stupored & dumb, fat-jointed in his joy.

I could go on like this
& probably will.
I could say fear of mice is called musophobia
& mysophobia is fear of dirt
& I have.
Tapinophobia is fear of being contagious,
I could say, and have
& also taphephobia, fear of cemeteries
& thanatophobia, fear of death.
Phobophobia, what else, fear of fear.

So many fears, fear of strangers, of change,
of blood, the forest, Germans, stepfathers.
Zoophobia, fear of animals & sociophobia, fear of friendship.
There's fear of darkness, of being seen, of infinity,
of being touched, of rain & of course verbophobia,
fear & dislike of words.

Where will this all end?
With mice who skid across your kitchen floor
& make you scream?
Your pug puppy is useless against mice.
Overcome with the wonder of it all
he plops onto his plump rump & chews his left back paw.
Logic is also useless
as is the pizza driver knocking on your door.

Even the Antarctica has its invasion
of the common house mouse
though pizzas are much harder to come by.

Fat or tall, mice learn. They climb trees, swim rivers
or shiver in tussock grass.
Rocks & bird eggs or power cables & trash,
airplanes all over the world huddle on runways
while cats are kept gainfully employed,
but life has meant so little since entire countries crumbled
at the touch of their scritchy, twitchy whiskers.

Stalin said *One death is a tragedy,*
one million a statistic. But what does that mean
when in AD 68, 10,000 Romans died each day.
A century later, two emperors, the entire Roman army
& sixteen years of Plague just begun.
100 million dead one rattled breath at a time.

One plus one plus one plus
1347—75 million in Europe, Asia, Africa.
1348—London. Nine out of every ten
& the children sang so sweetly
Ring around the rosie
Pocket full of posies
One last rattled breath plus one last rattled breath.
1850s—more than 11 million in India alone.
1899–1902—over 120 million.
1924—The Plague brought by sea-faring merchant mice & we're in Los Angeles.
1994—Again India.
We all fall down.
Now it is the year of terror, the new millennium
just begun & to where, to where
shall the small mouse lead them?

....

They say skeptical Symean threw his ring in the Nile—
a test—believing that if the Virgin Birth of Christ were true,
he'd recover his ring, and that night
he found it in the fish he was served for dinner.

Which works for me.
Any god should be as simple a thing
as mackerel in dill and butter,
as definite and definable as an all-night deli

and sixty-cent coffee and free refills
as long as you stay awake.
A god would have my back,
the ten thousand hammer slams of pain.

He would know the sudden grab and punch,
the iron bolt of fire
that twists down both legs' sciatica nerves
then slams out my big toes.

And he would draw water from the well for all the grandmas
who all their long lives have said not one word
against him and he'd heat it for them on the stove
and bust their wood and chop their corn patch too.

His shoe prints would have been found on the inside
of the locked fire escape doors of Hamlet's Imperial Foods.
He'd press his nose against the weave in the cotton mill
and suffer on slabs of what once were feet on the cold concrete.

With nothing but two ten-minute breaks and a half-hour lunch,
he'd stand in the corner with the loom
in the lint-whirled light fighting
through the grimed window high above his head

while whatever dreams he may have once had left him
to go on with their own miserable lives.

....

1.

It rained that day too
& the Tuscarawas lifted itself from winter
to smooth a gray blanket over the streets of Canton, Ohio,
a fog to which I had nothing to say three days after I ran away.

I was twelve & the winds came
& chased away the threat of flood
& later still he came & he was nice enough
to say please & to apologize for the cramped back seat.

Through the window over his shoulder I saw the pale branches
of the chestnut outlined like black wire against the full moon
which paled as it rose above the restless river
then hung itself in the tree tops.

So far, so cold, I whispered to myself, *like the streets,*
like the city. Like me. I promise.

2.

Well it was raining, you got that much right
but mixed with snow & I circled
my old man's Chevy kicking the slick tires
& making sure every time I went on the sidewalk
to break my mother's back.

My sister was crying, her stringy hair stuck to her wet cheeks.
The old man shouted from the house for her to shut up,
his words a salty block of ice I couldn't kick through. Her red ears,
my hands, nothing would ever get warm again.

I pulled her hair but she was too young
to know about getting away & screamed harder.
Hell I was too old for that.

I started up the road,
stepped on a crack & another & another.

3.

Nothing was alive not even the steam
shoving out of the sewage grates jeweled in ice.
That man was just in the wrong place
at the wrong time saying please
& sorry about his stinking car.

I laughed in his face, that busted hole of bad dreams,
started screaming before he was through.
He couldn't get his pants up fast enough
he was so scared & throwing money at me
like that would shut me up.

Yeah my name's Princess, there's a pea in my bed
& a double-edged dagger in my boot.

Yeah I'll break your heart;
now give it to me, all of it.

....

Long before the sun stutters
across the stubbled grass
my brother slumps over his black coffee,
the knotted fist in his back
from yesterday's clamor
with beams and steel to install wires,
pulleys, and tubes to bubble antibiotics
and feed to the chickens crowded
in pissy sawdust and ammonia-
choked air for some farmer
who might get sixteen cents a bird,
has not left his body.

His voice comes across rainless
fields over shriveled corn and wheat
where heat hangs like a sack of bones.
His voice in its rasp of exhaustion hangs.

More than two decades and he still won't talk
about the time our father held a pistol
against his head and beat him while I sat
not two feet away
knowing we were both going to die that night

or if he was ashamed
that though I was four years younger
I would point out mistakes
in his homework just as I don't say anything
about how I still get nosebleeds
because he couldn't stop until he saw blood.

What he does say is I don't know
what you're doing up there,
but if you need a job,

I can use you in the chicken houses.
I can put you to work.
Not like a dog, he adds.

And suddenly I'm overwhelmed
with the need to drive hundreds of miles
just to look at my brother
with his eyes that are black-rimmed from lack of sleep,
his sad and broken body,
but I don't say anything because after all
I know that what lies between us
is more than just miles
and it is me who is overcome with shame
that hours before I have even risen,
my brother's face is ashen with strain,
his hands cracked and swollen
and with those hands he tears himself
apart again and again.

....

It's one of those days lost in the coin-slotted way of loss,
cold-gullied and rainy so I've sought the scant heat
of the bus station with the others like this woman
who is worried about the Knicks; their stars grow old
and it's this year or never she tells me,

then pulls from her cord-handled bag
a baby blanket, straightens herself, rigid as a totem
and drapes it across her head.
I don't like it when the buses come in, she says
and grabs my arm as the whole terminal shudders.

I still wonder what happened to the Bulls
and the 'love of the game' clause
of Michael who shares a name with my brother
who is short and bent-back and too exhausted
for anything he may have ever loved.

It's enough. Don't ask about this middle-aged woman
who looks like a kid who forgot to cut eye-holes
for her Halloween costume except that instead of a white sheet
she has gone into the nightscare
with a blue teddy bear and buggy-bumper baby blanket.

Her grip tightens as the station shudders again
and who am I to complain at such a small need
especially since she's just told me I seem sweet,
offered to share her A&P three-day-old, dime-a-loaf bread
and some fruit she dug out of their dumpster,

Not bad bruised at all, she assures me,
if I'll only keep watch while she grabs some sleep.
Sleep easy I say, sleep if you can,
while the man the row of seats opposite
shouts at his buddies three rows down,

another homeless person has tried to rob him of—
I strain to hear over bus brakes and station-rustlings—a plate.
A door opens and dieseled growls
scuttle with wind and rain across the thin-tiled floor
and new pain claws up my arm

reminding me that we all grow old in this race toward the grave
and the pennant that's this year or never.
My brother used to live eight miles from Michael Jordan's parents.
He got phone calls all the time from hopeful teenagers
and once from an angry woman calling herself Shrug

and once from a kid and his mama
who were staying over Christmas at the battered women's shelter.
She kept saying *I told my son to go ahead and call that number,*
told him maybe there was hope after all,
but there was no hope, not for them, not even for Michael

when death opened his flea-gnawed wings and drifted down
to Michael's father murdered not three miles from my brother's house.
Dumped in a swamp, two fishermen found him stripped of ID
and his son's championship ring though the sheriff reported
that due to the fancy dental work *he knew he was somebody*

which is why they thought to save something for identification
and cut off his head and hands before cremating him.
It's odd how the dead come back to us,
nothing but head and hands
straight from the swamp with fish news and turtle news

and stories about the earth that trembles beneath feet,
islands that rise from water
and islands giving up in a gasp
of breath and bubbles and returning to water.
I wish for Michael that it weren't so

but they read his letters jealous for signs of his love,
they analyze that twist and mid-air turn and sail
listening for the ball-swoosh through net
that could only be a message to them
spread out from the nose-bleed seats to the VIP lounge.

I say to them, the man has only so many fingers
for so many championship rings;
don't visit his dreams wringing your empty hands.
Don't be like my dead, filling the air
with answers to questions he doesn't know to ask.

Don't open your mouth to show him
how the crows stole all your shiny fillings
and the baby alligators suckled from your gums.
If he dies rich with a ring for every finger
or a ragged ruin in a bus station

beside a woman with a blanket over her head,
don't say it means anything
because fact is no matter what the living do
you're still the unforgiving dead.
Hunched on these hard plastic seats silently crying out to God

to remember me there as I am surely forgotten here. I wish it so.
Just as I wish for the brother I never knew
the one before the anger
and fights and beatings, before the black beauties, coke, speed
and more speed, pink hearts, cross tabs, and pcp-dusted joints,

the one who could have found reason for a clause of love
and not just a job that beat him down
only to beat him down again.
For this woman beside me I wish a sleep
that doesn't fill with the screams of gang rapes

or police batons, one that never knows
the six-battery migraine-maker or the words *move on,*
easy sleep and an entire dumpster of fruit and bread, not stale.
And of course the Knicks all the way.
For the plate-thief, I wish a house full of plates

and the house to keep them in.
For the man across from me something like understanding
for though we never believe it,
we are a bruised and broken people,
wounds without salve, our small mouths

mouthing our small mantras—
plates and bread three days old and the Knicks—
for when this thing called death does not pass from us
what is one plate in a world not perfect but full of plates,
oh so, so full of plates.

....

I got cleaned up then: crabs, clap,
even my bladder infection though not drugs.
Drugs you score in jail easier than the streets.
Eighteen months of begging ex-girlfriends
to bring me clean underwear, change
for cigarettes & candy & I was out
& vowing to stay out.
From the soot & grime of Little Chicago
all the way to Florida I paced the Amtrak,
every window a framed photo
of sagging wires & squat houses
knowing I was dead. Already dead. & knowing it.

It was me what put that pimp PhillyBoy behind bars.
Three years, they give him & each blasted minute screaming my name.

...

In Florida I thought to myself *so this is America.*
Palm trees swayed in wind like the last dancers
at a midnight ball, music poured
into the streets & people offered long-stem roses
to the sky & waltzed with strangers & were not afraid.
But I was as afraid as ever

& hated men even more.
Black men, white men, Hispanics,
that cop back in Ohio who arrested me;
he waited until I was on my knees
mouth full of cock before he flashed
his smirk & his badge.

I left teeth marks on him. He left me bruised,
a deep months-long ache, but not so it'd show.

. . .

You don't get out of that life, not alive.
I paced the streets
with a knife's edgy smile in my boot.
Every car kept watch, every loud sound, fatal.
My final ragged breath
waited around the next building
& when he found me   & he would find me
his hands would not forget how to erase all evidence.

I'm telling you I've seen the rooms
where women are kept the few days it takes
strung out on drugs & begging
to use the bathroom & I know what happens
when the pimp says no & above all I know the line
of men, the number of times they're fucked.

. . .

I don't have a story.   Nothing
about economics or sexual freedom or choice.

What I have is Shelly—Star, beaten to death by a john;
LaTonya—Sugar Mama, drug overdose; Amy—Candy,
gone, disappeared,   dead;   I have
Teresa, shot by a john; Elyce—raped
& raped & raped again—her insides bled right out of her;
Sandra—Hepatitis C; Catherine—booze;
Marie—ice, meth, smack, crack; Laura, Lisa, Jenny, Mary Anne,
all dead—Acquired Immune Deficiency Syndrome;
Darla—who knows, just went mad on us;
& Shannon, ovarian cancer.

What I have is how I shed each night's silent screams
like skin until I'm stripped raw & still screaming.

...

Florida where I was as afraid as ever
& hated even more. Men
& the way their penises grow hard
at a couple of beers & some faint
resemblance to some childhood centerfold fantasy.

I knew it was time; fear kept at me, coiling around
its own long string of slime until there was nothing left.
If he had followed me,   which he had
it didn't matter   I was already erased. I ran again
& again   & finally to here, right back on the streets,

crack's eight-eyed stare never letting me alone, a whore once
a whore forever, strung between that other world & mine,
the tangle of my life with nowhere to go because once you've entered
The Golden Pheasant, there's no leaving & no return.

....

The way something will define us
though we never know it:

brooding sun, wasp-drone, fat-headed bumblebees
bumping against drought-shrunk ragweed,

the day itchy as a ghost limb,

we all laughing at the banty-legged boy
bragging about standing on a water barrel
and diddling his horse and when he said
he changed his sister's diaper and put it in her too,
we never said a word.

We were young and infant sisters ourselves,
pink and thin-skinned, swimming our way through summer,
delicate as spiders, curved as egg sacs ready to spill.
We thought yesterday was a sad song,

nothing worth our bodies' attachments,
thought nobody would remember a twelve-year-old boy
bragging about mounting his horse and his baby sister.
Certainly not the baby sister.

We didn't know then how we forget nothing.

Didn't know that what our minds put aside
our bodies clench tight.
Tapped and tagged by the unseen and unremembered
sun-freckled in our pink one-piece suits we wait
sketched in, sketched out, daubed and washed and washed
and still nothing

to tell us how that which we never quite see

takes our hand and leads us stone by stone
across the creek and lifts us onto her shoulders
to paddle the sun-dappled apple leaves with our sticky fists.

What does this have to do with the slow night
here at the pizza joint, the phones ringing
somewhere, ringing and ringing,
                                                  but not here?

It's just one of the things our minds give us,
part of the past with its nameless faces and free beers
waiting for us up ahead no matter what prayers
we surround ourselves with in the insect-humming air.

And tonight? Angelo, youngest Greek brother,
only two months in the country, dumped
the morning after he and his girl's first night.
Big Mike, second generation,
dispensing advice like a pharmacist.

He holds out one cupped hand,
here you have the hair, the lips,
his voice drops and they huddle closer
until Angelo leaps backward and says
I not do that. I no put my mouth there.

Of course I say it: *we know why you got dumped,*
how could I resist, and they close in again
despite my offer, as the only woman in the room,
to hook them up with the inside info.

Maybe this is where I'm supposed to get upset,
but truth is I'm fascinated
by people's fascination with sex.

Besides it's a slow night,
a game of waiting
for the sun to go down, the heat to break,
and frat boys to get drunk,
a five-gallon pickle bucket makes a good seat

and I think it's sweet when men slam back
and give each other pointers,
Big Mike saying you've got to go down on her,
got to, got to,
it's what they expect, American women.

Or just last week when I had to wait
in a dank frat room while a brother demonstrated
to a dozen others. *Thrust, twist, and pause,*
he said, shoving the words through air with his entire arm
and hips and body. *Thrust,* his whole arm shoving up,
twist, a quick wrist-fist flick and swiveled hip,
and pause, before saying it again, *Thrust, twist, and pause,*

until it became a chant,
a prayer
for him to turn to

no matter what the first scour of light brought
and me standing there, his pizza sweating into the cup of my palm.
It works, he said, then with a glance at me,
at least my girlfriend likes it.

So she says,

I thought, and maybe
while he wrote out the check
I should have told him about the G-spot, the flick of tongue,

angle and moves of the fingers of one hand, pressure
and place just above the pubic bone for the other
but instead I opt for the safe and sure,
a buck tip.

Besides, why should men have to do all the work?

When have I ever said to a woman over a glass of red wine,
Do you know the Taoist method of male multiple orgasm
for him to come again and again?
Or even the last second hard squeeze? No? Feigned surprise.
And you wonder why the Villa parking lot is packed with hookers
making money for their pimps who shoot pool in the deli basement
though there's no money tonight for the drivers who still wait
while they try to convince Angelo he must
go down on a woman, he insisting Greeks don't do that,
Chimbukee yes, he says, *but 68 and I owe you one.*

This dismays me; the hot-blooded Mediterranean lover
just another myth
winging off into the wavering sky

then my mind in one of its perv twists
leaps to all those bars
where beer-breathed I straddled a stool past last call,
then chose
from the unchosen one face to pull to mine.

If it was winter I carried a Rohm .22 in my coat
or in a backpack if it was warm
and almost was never afraid.
I rose first and checked the mail for the name
I would have forgotten.

Cold water smelling of chemicals and iron splashed
across my face. This for a bed,
toast and eggs or at least dry cereal, a beer.

How far away those days are now when I lie down
in the rain-leaking, rusty indifference of my pickup
and wake to back pain so thorough
it lifts me, scrubbed clean from myself,
                                                                                    then drops me
back to this place, specific in its heat-hazed loneliness.

                                                                                    So it goes;
we all have our ghosts.

This man, for instance, hunched
in the thread of his jacket here in the parking lot,
smoke curling from his fingers,
telling me he used to catch the trains.
Rode one all the way to Chicago once.

Plenty of room up under 'em. You can sit up,
lie down, love a woman. He winks, throws an elbow,
Hey spare a dollar. What do you say baby?
We can get a six-pack. Hey, hey, help me out.

And why should I be upset?
          a matter of degree between him
and my nameless faces
                                                  the past waiting
even for Angelo who finally says *OK.*
I will do it.   *I am Greek no more.*

But of course he is. Born in that strange land,
                                                                                                  die in that strange land

where so many brothers have planted their dead,
world of wounded, ravaged light,
the raging, toothy sun under which everything is set fire,
all of Greece and its people burning.

....

Look here, you best better do something about them there bruises.
No man want a woman look like she already been used
in no good way. You try some baking soda and seltzer water
on that there blood. It's the only thing I know what works.
Look here, who cares, a man see you looking like that
and all he's gonna think is about doing you more the same.
You ain't needing no more of that; not tonight no how.
Aww look, the moon, how pretty. What kind of tree is that anyhow
and that moon just hanging there like a balloon
done got stuck up in them there branches.
Why look, ain't that there your regular, and Salt
and Pepper climbing up in his back seat.
I guess even that one, times he needs him something different.
Yeah baby, soda and seltzer. Might work. Rub it right out, that blood.

....

How close we are
                                        how stingy
though we slog slash-mouthed through the mud-beach of our own stories
sunk in the slow blue of solitude.

How useless our words
when the mimosa folds its bony fingers
and the spindly-limbed chinaberry
fumbles its small harvest.

Yes in this flawed world there is a past
but what does it mean to us,
                                                        huddled here
salveless misers of our own little hoards of hurt
unable to forgive ourselves the smallest sins.

There's a reason why yesterday in rain and no wind
the oak under which I parked my truck
lifted its tangled roots from the earth
and hung slant-wise in bleared air
then slowly toppled to the ground;
a reason
            but I don't know it.

I don't know why cotton blooms pink, yellow, and blue;
I've never taken the ferry up the narrow canal to Poros,
never seen the black-bearded priests on their donkeys,
the white-washed houses piled on each other like steps.

Never walked the narrow cobblestone between plazas of gnarled olive
or seen the orange trees blinking against the sun,
almonds waiting in their caskets of green fuzz,
never seen oystercatchers winging in air
or the drowned skin divers laid out on sand.

I don't know the flocks of goats chased from the runway
only what I've been told.
In this world of words, imperfect, but all we have,
I've never seen the sea caves of Corfu shimmered in color,
but rows of tobacco in bled dirt where nothing else grows.

Don't know the donkey paths between villages in morning mist
only the stories people tell.

Not the burnished Acropolis in mythical light
but fields in drought and flood,
nights when bootleggers stay home,
moaning trees in wind, moon down,
something forgotten walking the damp woods,
some thing forgotten, walking.

NOTES

Távla sto meϑeési (p. 3). Blind drunk.

Me léne Kóstas (p. 3). My name is Kostas.

The town which is now a field (p. 4). Of 6,500 villages, 1,400 were burned during the occupation, and 500 were completely destroyed.

To écho se kakó (p. 5). I think it is a bad omen.

Akrotiri (p. 6). The Lost Atlantis.

Onomázome Kóstas (p. 18). My name is Kostas.

The years of occupation (p. 23). Of the 72,606 Jews living in Greece, 58,600 were deported by Germans and 4,212 by Bulgarians. Eight hundred escaped to the Middle East and 8,000 joined the guerrillas. The rest were hidden in homes. Only a few thousand of those sent to Germany survived and returned to Greece after the war.

Kalávryta (p. 24). The entire male population of the town was shot. The women and children were forced into barns to which the German soldiers set fire.

Athens, February, 1942 (p. 29). In the four years of occupation by Germans, Italians, and Bulgarians, approximately 900,000 Greek civilians died, many from starvation.

Horta (p. 29). Edible wild green.

Hymettus (p. 29).	Mountain in Athens.
ELAS (p. 30).	Military arm of EAM, a Communist political party.
Miserias, Aris (p. 30).	Pseudonym for Thanassis Kloras, leader of ELAS.
Kapetanios (p. 30).	Chieftain, military rank of leader, Miserias.
Antares (p. 30).	Communist guerrilla soldiers.

•••••••••

Sixty-Cent Coffee and a Quarter to Dance is set around a time of my life when, although employed by a Greek-owned restaurant, I was often homeless. My homelessness was mostly due to the high rent in the area and the difficulty in meeting day-to-day bills while saving enough money for first and last month's rent as well as a security deposit, and also due to medical bills from a severely herniated disc that eventually led to (surgery-corrected) paralysis. While the "working girls" in the parking lot, the other restaurant workers, and the other homeless with whom I shared coffee refills and the warmth of bus station terminals, and, of course, "Chris" all represent the failures of the past century and of the socioeconomic policies of the United States, this poem is only my personal encounter with and representation of those failures. This poem is full of other people's stories, other people's words as they were told to me. I do not imagine that I can fully represent anyone else's experiences of the past century and indeed the poem speaks to the hopelessness of complete understanding and communication, but also to the imperativeness of an attempt at empathy, understanding, communication, and more.